WRNS
IN CAMERA

WRNS
IN CAMERA

LESLEY THOMAS AND CHRIS HOWARD BAILEY

Royal Naval
MUSEUM
Publications

SUTTON PUBLISHING

First published in the United Kingdom in 2002 by
Sutton Publishing Limited · Phoenix Mill
Thrupp · Stroud · Gloucestershire · GL5 2BU
In association with the Royal Naval Museum

British Library Cataloguing in Publication Data
A catalogue record for this book is available from the British Library.

ISBN 0-7509-1370-3

Half-title page photograph: A Wireless Telegraphist talks to a pilot on a test flight, *c.* 1943. (Lee Miller Archive, 5790–38)

Frontispiece: A group of Radio Telegraphy Operators under training, *c.* 1941. (Courtesy of the Fleet Air Arm Museum, Crown Copyright)

Title-page photograph: Happy 21st Birthday! The WRNS celebrated the occasion in 1960 with a series of parades through towns and cities across the UK and overseas. The WRNS units in Portsmouth marched through the city, taking the salute as they passed the Guildhall. (RNM, 1/90 (56))

Endpapers. Front: A Boarding Officer in action, *c.* 1942. (RNM, 24/91 (175))

Back: Visual Signaller Wrens signalling to ships of the Allied invasion force, June 1944. (RNM, 350/88 (170*33))

Typeset in 11/15pt Baskerville MT.
Typesetting and origination by
Sutton Publishing Limited.
Printed and bound in England by
J.H. Haynes & Co. Ltd, Sparkford.

CONTENTS

Lee Miller was an accredited war photographer with the US Army. Having been employed as a fashion photographer for *Vogue* magazine, she was interested in women working with the armed forces. In Britain she was allowed unlimited access to naval establishments on the south coast and photographed Wrens going about their work. (Lee Miller Archive, 4998–26)

FOREWORD

Formal and reportage portraits of officers and politicians are notably rare in Lee Miller's work. She was much more interested in celebrating ordinary people doing extraordinary things in an ordinary way. On her many assignments with the Women's Royal Naval Service (WRNS) she formed an immediate rapport with these women sailors. Her own pre-war experience as a photographer enabled her to understand better than most the difficulties they experienced working in a male-dominated world. She respected their skills, their tenacity and their willingness to face the very real dangers of the sea and the enemy. According to those who met her, the Wrens took a similar liking to Lee, and this is self-evident in the photographs. The intimacy of some of the studies shows a trust on both sides, and a shared sense of purpose. Lee takes care to record events faithfully, but at the same time her artistic flair brings out the best in every face in every situation. She shows us the quiet heroism of their self-sacrifice. She shows the competence and professionalism, the humour and the comradeship that were everyday currency among these people.

In Lee's photograph on p. ix the marching Wrens file away from the camera, anonymity blanketing their individuality, with helmets and gas-mask cases taking the place of hats and handbags. In her later shots Lee reasserts their personalities as they appear in all their different roles. She reminds us this is a force composed of women who succeeded in releasing men to fight by replacing them in non-combatant roles one for one: the dangerous workshop jobs done in filthy conditions, the bravely borne tedium, the quiet concentration of radio operators, or the caring, almost maternal look on the faces of the quarter-master teams and the instructors. We see the dignity of the Wrens in their many roles and we capture something of the spirit of their time. We even meet some officers, as Vera Laughton Mathews, Director WRNS (p. 8) and First Officer Esta Eldod (p. 71) clearly won Lee's respect and affection.

Lee Miller began photographing Wrens in September 1941 at HMS *Heron*, the Fleet Air Arm base in Yeovil. Her work was first published as an article titled *Seaworthy and Semi Seagoing* in the September 1943 issue of *Vogue* magazine with text by Leslie Blanch, and then as a book by Lee Miller titled *Wrens in Camera*, published by Hollis & Carter in 1945. The delay in publication was as much due to paper shortages as to Lee's absence in Europe covering the advance of the US Army across Europe.

Very little was known about some of the extraordinary work done by Wrens during the war. Lee Miller was keen to record some of the more unusual tasks and here is preparing to photograph two Torpedo Wrens. (Lee Miller Archive, 4998–54)

The artistry of Lee Miller is evident in this photograph of Wrens marching to their place of work, *c.* 1942. (Lee Miller Archive, 4078–24)

Lee Miller's sense of form highlights a Wren on watch, *c.* 1943. (Lee Miller Archive, 5208–20)

Lee Miller was allowed to take pictures in places that were off-limits to other photographers. Here an Amenities Liaison Wren, a category introduced in 1941, is working in a liaison library, a facility providing recreational resources, such as books and records, for sailors and Wrens, *c.* 1942. (Lee Miller Archive, 5208–7)

The example of the Wrens cannot fail to inspire anyone who studies them and their achievements. This book, also fittingly titled *WRNS in Camera*, is not principally about a war; it is about a group of remarkable women who united to overcome social, physical and technical difficulties and in doing so triumphed but were only fleetingly acknowledged at the time. With its many fine additional photographs by Royal Navy photographers and others, including amateurs, assembled with great care by Lesley Thomas (a former Wren herself) and Dr Chris Howard Bailey, it is a fitting tribute to the WRNS. This new version of *WRNS in Camera* goes a long way towards redressing the shameful lack of acknowledgement they have endured. Above all, it is an expression of our debt of gratitude.

Antony Penrose
The Lee Miller Archive
www.leemiller.co.uk

PREFACE

The photographic content of the following chapters reflects the diversity and, in some cases, the unusual and unexpected nature of the work carried out by Wrens during the Second World War. Every single woman who served in the WRNS, regardless of the work she did, played an important part in helping the Royal Navy in its contribution to the successful outcome of the war.

The Domestic Branch, reflecting its importance, became the third largest in the Service. Originally the Admiralty Board thought that only a small number of unskilled Cooks and Stewards would be needed but their numbers grew to many thousands, with the Director, Mrs Vera Laughton Mathews, insisting that the Cooks, because of the nature and importance of their work, must be regarded as skilled workers. The Stewards and other Domestic Branch workers, such as Hall Porters and Laundrymaids and so on, were just as important to the maintenance of WRNS quarters and naval wardrooms.

Wrens employed in the Clerical and Supply Branches assisted by ensuring that the WRNS itself was run efficiently and they were also responsible for the smooth running of many naval departments and supply depots. They formed two of the largest branches, reflecting the huge demand for their services. As the war progressed, and more and more men were needed to serve at sea, it was not unusual for some offices and depots to be run and staffed entirely by Wrens.

The rapid introduction of new technology during the war led to changes in the work of large numbers of Wrens. This was especially true of the Technical trades, which included engineering, mechanics and electronics, plus many other specialisations. More and more Wrens were employed in areas that were previously considered to be unsuited to women. However, demand soon outstripped scepticism and the work of the Technical Wrens proved vital to the repair, maintenance and successful operation of almost every kind of naval equipment.

Wrens in the Communications Branch played a pivotal role in every area of communications. They were especially important in the months before and during Operation Neptune, the naval element of the D-Day operations. In some cases entire communications centres were run and operated by WRNS personnel and they were responsible for sending and receiving thousands of important signals every day. The varied nature of the work in this branch, from radio and radar to wireless telegraphy and signalling with flags, meant that the Wrens were often working with new technologies and could be found in lonely outposts in some of the furthest regions of the UK and abroad.

The Fleet Air Arm drew its Wrens from all branches but especially from the Supply, Technical and Communications Branches. Their skills and expertise were put to use on air stations all over the UK and overseas and they were given the hugely important task of being responsible for the airworthiness of the aircraft and all the equipment used on board. Others were involved in training pilots and aircrews or were responsible for aircraft movements on and off the air stations.

Thousands of Wrens worked in categories or trades that did not fall within the main branches. The rapid expansion of the Service and the demand for Wrens trained in new and varied roles began to outstrip the formal structure of job classification. Varying in numbers from several thousands to very often just a few, perhaps five or ten, they were employed in areas as varied as gardening, foundry work, driving, mail delivery, boat maintenance, welfare work and numerous others. Many worked with the Fleet Air Arm, the Royal Marines, Coastal Forces and Combined Operations, and regardless of the less-well-known nature of their work, and their smaller numbers, they were as important to the war effort as the larger and better-known trades.

Most of the women, especially the teenagers, who joined the WRNS during the war were experiencing life away from home for the first time. For quite a few thousand there was the additional excitement of being sent to serve overseas. Demand was such that by September 1944 there were nearly 5,000 Wrens serving in Europe, the Mediterranean, North America, North and South Africa, Southern India, Ceylon and Australia. They were drawn from all categories, the largest numbers being Communications and Clerical Wrens, but the work of every Wren who served overseas was invaluable and provided each with an experience that for most was unique and unforgettable.

Over 75,000 Wrens served during the Second World War. Every single one, regardless of the type of work she did, made a vital contribution to the WRNS and to the Royal Navy. The following chapters are a tribute to those women who, along with their female comrades in the other Services and in civilian life, made such a difference to the war effort.

CHAPTER ONE

INTRODUCTION

Since 1990 all female officers and ratings joining the Royal Navy have been liable for sea service as a condition of entry.[1] This was a radical change of policy that many, both inside and outside the Service, thought would never work. Key figures in the Admiralty and the Civil Service had argued that it would work *eventually* and pushed for its introduction.[2] Yet despite the challenges of such a change in policy, and the great difficulties the first women subject to this change encountered, the opposition appears gradually to have subsided. After twelve years many of the teething troubles have been resolved and by the end of 2001 there were just under a thousand women serving in seagoing billets. There are fifty-two ships with female crew members, who on average make up 10–15 per cent of a ship's company. This includes 136 officers, 34 senior rates and 734 junior ratings among the embarked personnel. Almost all posts in the Royal Navy are open to women, with the exception of the Submarine Service, the Royal Marine Commando and Mine Clearance Diving (although women can qualify as ship's divers).

The acceptance of integration has not been without difficulties. The initial public reaction to 'dual-manning' was somewhat alarmist. The media in particular was hostile and sought the sensational. It responded to the news of the introduction of dual-manning by focusing almost entirely on the sexual challenges faced by the young men and women working and living together in confined, close quarters. The headlines were lurid: 'Dressed to Kill, Gulf Veterans Uneasy Over Wrens on Ships' and 'Sex and the Services: Mixing Men and Women in the New Age Navy Requires Not Only Rules, but a Subtle Code of Sexual Etiquette'. Such headlines in turn aggravated the anxieties some young naval wives had about the situation.[3] The response of some wives was extreme, but most men in the Royal Navy were sceptical. One officer writing in *The Naval Review*, for example, although lamenting adverse publicity for the WRNS, challenged the decision to send women to sea, fearing men will always respond to women, as 'they have over the centuries' with 'a gallantry, not condescension, naturally

1. Minister of State for the Armed Forces, The Rt Hon Archie Hamilton MP, February 1990.
2. Oral history interview with Admiral Sir Brian Brown KCB, CBE, Second Sea Lord 1988–91 (RNM Oral History Collection 456/1993).
3. See, for example, Kate Muir, *The Times Saturday Review*, 13 April 1991, pp. 4–6; David Cragg, *The News* (Portsmouth), 24 October 1991, p. 2; Sara Barrett, *Daily Mail*, 2 April 1992, p. 23; Kate Muir, *The Times*, 9 August 1992, p. 12.
4. Aeneas, 'The Employment of Women in the Royal Navy: A Retrospective', *The Naval Review* 79 (October 1991), pp. 328–34. (Some of this material also appeared in an article, 'Ambassadors of England: Work and Leisure for the Wrens in Malta 1944–1950', published in the *Oral History Journal*, Autumn 1993, pp. 55–64.)

expected of [them]'.[4] The author of the article was concerned that the anticipated dual standards imposed on the men and women serving together would undermine the close-knit community known as the ship's company.

However, in the years since dual-manning was first mooted, the Navy has worked hard to overcome prejudice and hostile reactions. Its equal opportunities awareness training has been instrumental in improving attitudes. Continuous and on-going research by the Royal Navy into all aspects of sea service shows that women have become accepted as crew members on mixed-manned ships and, importantly, are not regarded as detrimental to the operational effectiveness of their ships.

The gradual public and institutional acceptance of women as an integral and equal component of the Royal Navy's personnel owes much to the changing values and beliefs of society in general. Women have struggled generally to become more visible and self-aware in what was once a dominant male-defined culture.[5] Women, of course, have always worked, as Alice Kessler-Harris has ably demonstrated: 'Women have always worked – in their homes and in the homes of others, in fields, in factories, shops, stores and offices . . . what remains the same is that the ways in which women have worked involve a constant struggle between two areas of lives: the home and the marketplace'.[6] What *has* changed over the years is the integration of women in a world of work in which most jobs were defined as a male province. Gender stereotyping in the workplace, while it very much still exists, has been gradually eroded. This has been so in society at large and it is no less so in the Royal Navy.

Importantly, the earlier pioneering work of the WRNS and the role of the Wrens in both peace and war paved the way for the erosion of such stereotyping in the Royal Navy. The women in the WRNS have always had to overcome limiting definitions of their potential and it was the exigencies and demands of war, particularly the Second World War, which enabled them to forge new understandings and acceptances of their capabilities. This book aims to illustrate, through a series of striking images from the Lee Miller Archive and the Royal Naval Museum Photographic Collection, the divergent and sometimes contradictory roles of the Wrens during the Second World War. Significantly, it will reveal the extent of tasks undertaken by women in the Service and show how much of what is happening to women in the Navy now was first experienced by the grandmothers of the present generation.

Origins of the WRNS

The Women's Royal Naval Service was initially formed during the First World War, in November 1917, as a response to a 'deterior-ating manpower situation in the Navy'.[7] The intention was to employ women in domestic and clerical jobs, such as Cooks, Waitresses, Clerks, Writers and Telephonists, in order to release men for sea service.[8] Their slogan was 'Never at Sea'.[9] As the war developed,

5. See the work of Sheila Rowbotham, who has outlined many of these changes; particularly, *A Century of Women: The History of Women in Britain and the United States* (New York, Viking, 1997).
6. Alice Kessler-Harris, *Women Have Always Worked: An Historical Overview* (New York, McGraw-Hill Book Company, 1981).
7. Ursula Stuart Mason, *The Wrens 1917–77* (Reading, Educational Explorers, 1977).
8. Commandant M.H. Fletcher WRNS, *The WRNS: A History of The Women's Royal Naval Service* (London, B.T. Batsford Ltd, 1989), p. 13.
9. In addition to the Mason and Fletcher accounts of the early years of the WRNS see also: *The Wrens – Being the Story of their Beginnings and Doings in Various Parts, 1917–1919* (London, WRNS Headquarters, 1919); Eileen Bigland, *The Story of The W.R.N.S.*

however, so did the nature of their jobs and the women proved equally adept at tasks once thought to be the preserve of men. For example, they repaired searchlights, cleaned mines and primed depth-charges.[10] They became plumbers, engineers and electricians and one even 'captained'[11] a motor launch while others became stokers.[12] But when the Armistice was declared, it was reasoned that there was no longer any need to retain the Service and so, despite their enormous contributions and successes, the WRNS was finally disbanded in October 1919.

When the Second World War became imminent in 1938, the WRNS was re-formed. The initial plan was to employ the women once again in mainly clerical and domestic jobs – seemingly the experience of the First World War was forgotten – so that they could release the men to fight. Again, however, the exigencies of war allowed the women to overcome the restrictions placed on them and they were able to engage in a variety of non-traditional roles. As Commandant Fletcher said: 'They were to prove themselves capable of coping with dangerous and difficult circumstances, developing considerable endurance, turning their hands to an infinite variety of tasks and earning a reputation for high standards and loyalty to the Royal Navy.'[13]

Recruitment and Training

When the Second World War began in 1939, events began to move quite quickly. The recruiting of large numbers of women began almost immediately. By May 1940 a Superintendent (Recruiting) was appointed to the staff of the Director WRNS and she was supported by a Travelling Recruiting Officer for the Midlands and North of England and later by another who was responsible for recruiting in Scotland.

In December 1941 the National Service Act (i.e. national conscription) was applied to women and the three women's services came to be regarded as part of the Armed Services of the Crown. This became law in March 1942 and thereafter any woman between the ages of twenty and thirty could be called into one of the women's services. Successful recruiting had led to long waiting lists to join the WRNS and by December 1941 conscription was restricted so that women were recruited generally rather than enlisting for specific jobs. Wrens chosen for specific jobs or 'categories' had to have appropriate, minimum educational qualifications such as School Certificate Credit in Mathematics or Physics, general German language skills or practical experience of boat work. However, special consideration could be given for admittance to the Service, if agreed by the Director WRNS – for example, previous service in the WRNS or having other family members who had served or were serving in the Royal or Merchant Navies. Importantly, though, all National Service Wrens were required to be 'Mobile', which meant they had no choice in where they served.[14]

Competition to get into the WRNS during the Second World War was very strong. As Waller and Vaughan-Rees noted: 'The WRNS, from quite early on, was the hardest to get into; at their wartime peak they numbered no more than 74,000, compared with 170,000 Women's Auxiliary Air Force

(London, Nicholson and Watson, 1946); John G. Drummond, *Blue For A Girl: The Story of The W.R.N.S.* (London, W.H. Allen, 1960); Katharine Furse, *Hearts and Pomegranates: The Story of Forty-Five Years, 1875–1920* (London, Peter Davies, 1940); Vera Laughton Mathews, *Blue Tapestry* (London, Hollis and Carter, 1949).
10. Mason, *The Wrens*, p. 33.
11. Mason, *The Wrens*, p. 41.
12. Mason, *The Wrens*, p. 37.
13. Fletcher, *The WRNS*, p. 26.
14. BR 1076.

(WAAF) and 198,000 Auxiliary Territorial Service (ATS).'[15] The medical requirements for entry were also quite stringent. For ratings, for example: 'The standard of fitness for entry into the WRNS will normally be Grade I. Candidates placed in Grade II may be accepted provided their physical defects are either remedial before call-up or are covered by paragraph 8 of this article. . . .' (Paragraph 8 stated that the defects were to be of a dental or visual nature or some such defect that could be corrected.) The final judgement lay with the Medical Officers.[16]

Similarly, very high standards of conduct were expected from recruits, who had to show respect to their superior officers and strict obedience to their orders:

> Every person in the Women's Royal Naval Service is to conduct herself with the utmost respect to her superior officer and with strict obedience to his or her orders; she is at all times to discharge every part of her duty with zeal and alacrity and to strive to promote the interest of the Naval Service. . . . Every member will on all occasions endeavour to uphold the honour of the WRNS and by the good order and regularity of her conduct prove herself worthy of the Service to which she belongs. . . . WRNS in uniform are not to indulge in noisy or rowdy behaviour in public, [nor] loiter around the men's quarters, workshops, parade grounds or dockyard gates.[17]

In order to determine whether women were suitable for the Service, they were put on a strict two-week probationary period, but 'in exceptional circumstances this [was] extended to a month as a maximum'.[18] During this time they underwent quite arduous basic training:

Square bashing was drill squad. We were taken out early in the morning, it seemed, to do this drill on the parade ground, and, of course, we were in divisions and wearing new issue shoes. Not funny! We had lectures; we had to light the schoolroom fire which often found me in tears on my knees, because I couldn't get the thing to go; damp wood I expect. We were there for two weeks and then we could make up our minds whether we wanted to stay or not.[19]

If they survived this stage, they went on to complete their trade training. This rigorous induction period served to reinforce a sense of belonging to a choice group – select, elite and privileged to be chosen to serve their country:

> We had all these different forms we had to memorise, all these accounting pro-cedures, and we had exams, etc. [If] you flopped, you were chucked out, you know. There was no going back. . . . The other Wrens used to go out and about in the evenings and enjoy themselves, and I stayed behind with the naval manual swotting, and I came second from the top at the exam, so I was quite pleased with myself.[20]

By the last quarter of 1942 there was a serious shortage of recruits. Due to earlier restrictions

15. Jane Waller and Michael Vaughan-Rees, *Women in Uniform, 1939–1945* (London, Papermac, 1989), p. 6.
16. BR 1077 (1), Regulations and Instructions for the Women's Royal Naval Service to 31 December 1943, p. 65.
17. BR 1077 (1), p. 7.
18. BR 1077 (1), p. 66.
19. Jeanne Culver, Cypher Wren, Interview, 30 April 1992, RNM OHC, 167/92.
20. Peggy Stoker, Supply Wren, Interview, 28 April 1992, RNM OHC, 169/92.

there was a shortfall of 12,000 Wrens but conditions had now changed. There was a tremendous need to use men and women economically; general training for recruits had been introduced and the growth of Technical categories necessitated central training centres being set up in thirteen towns around the country. By April 1943 a remarkable turnaround in the numbers being recruited meant that once again restrictions were introduced and this was achieved, in part, by raising the entry standards for certain Technical categories. Towards the end of the war only a small number of recruits were allowed to join the WRNS. They were mainly Stewards and Cooks, although some joined Technical categories. The Service had no difficulty getting such recruits. By the end of 1945 only three thousand were needed and by 1946 this number had halved. After this the level was regarded as 'sufficient to meet the new requirements'.[21]

Conditions of Service

Initially, at the beginning of the Second World War, three areas of employment were proposed for the Women's Royal Naval Service: the Office Duties Branch, the Motor Transport Branch and the General Duties Branch (Cooks, Stewards, Waitresses, Managers, Orderlies, etc.). As well as the 'Mobile' class of women willing to serve anywhere, there was an 'Immobile' class who would only serve in their immediate neighbourhood. For financial reasons this was considered an expedient classification because it cost less to have women living at home than in hostels but there were also social and political considerations that influenced the decision. All the women were to be British subjects or born of British parents and aged between eighteen and forty-five. They were to be granted sick leave and assigned relative naval rank for the purposes of allowances, injury or death compensation but were not granted equivalent naval rank or rating. Nor were they to be allowed to wear the distinguishing rank of naval officers. The uniform was to be the same as that of the First World War but with changes to reflect the fashion of the times. Ratings were to be paid a flat rate with a small addition according to duties and officers were paid from £200 per annum for Second Officers, £240 for First Officers and £280 for Chief Officers. Those who had to serve away from home were given small additional allowances. The Deputy Director and Port Superintendents were offered £500 per year and the Director £750. They were also offered pensions. Importantly, though, the women were not subject to the Naval Discipline Act.[22]

In order to release a man for sea service it was agreed that, in general terms, one naval rating would be replaced by one member of the WRNS. The four Commands at Plymouth, Portsmouth, Chatham and Rosyth established that they would need a total of 131 WRNS Administrative Officers. By the time war was declared 220 of these WRNS officers were distributed over the four Commands.[23] By the end of the war there were 9,743 at most of the naval bases and establishments throughout the United Kingdom.[24]

21. BR 1076, p. 51.
22. BR 1076, p. 16.
23. BR 1076, p. 61.
24. BR 1076, pp. 63–4.

Dame Katharine Furse, Director WRNS, 1919
Dame Katharine Furse was appointed as Director of the newly created Women's Royal Naval Service (WRNS) in November 1917. She was previously the Chief Commandant of the Red Cross-run Voluntary Aid Detachments (VADs) and was regarded as an ideal leader for the fledgling Service. (RNM, 350/88 (155*1)

Wrens at Granton Naval Base, 1918
The WRNS was created in November 1917 and its numbers grew very rapidly. Some naval bases had significant numbers of Wrens working on them. This mixed group of officers and ratings consists of Domestic, Clerical and Technical workers. (RNM, 68/88 (C49))

A group of Wrens being demobbed, 1919
The WRNS was only in existence for nineteen months, with demobilisation beginning in November 1918 and, owing to the large numbers involved, not finishing until almost a year later in October 1919. These Household Workers belonged to a category that consisted of more than twenty different jobs. (RNM, 447/89 (2))

Portrait photograph by Lee Miller of Mrs Vera Laughton Mathews, Director WRNS 1939–47
Mrs Laughton Mathews was an ideal choice as Director WRNS having served as the WRNS Unit Officer at the Crystal Palace Training Depot in 1918–19. She was personally recommended by her predecessor, Dame Katharine Furse, who recognised her leadership qualities. (Lee Miller Archive)

Early days at WRNS HQ in the Admiralty Building, 1939

When the re-formation of the WRNS was announced in the autumn of 1939, WRNS Headquarters, which had been set up in a small back room at the Admiralty in London, was inundated with thousands of applications to join the Service. Here the first HQ staff sort through the mountains of requests. (RNM, 350/88 (170*45))

Mill Hill WRNS Training Depot, London, 1942

The WRNS expanded so quickly that standardisation of training was urgently needed but there was a serious shortage of suitable accommodation for so many new-entry Wrens. In March 1942 the Mill Hill Depot was opened as the central training and accommodation depot for all new-entry 'Mobile' Wrens. It housed 900 women and was in continuous use until February 1946 except for a temporary closure in 1944 because of the risk posed by air raids. (RNM, 1/90 (26))

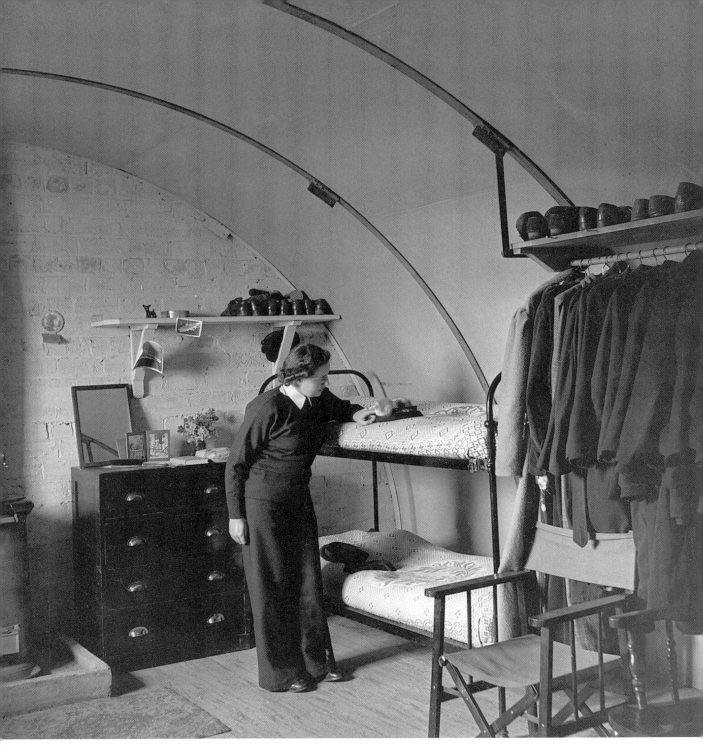

A Wren in typical accommodation, *c.* **1942**
WRNS accommodation varied greatly in both location and quality. Some were lucky enough to live in requisitioned stately homes, private schools or hotels but for other Wrens the quality was poorer, especially on outlying stations in remote areas. (Lee Miller Archive, 5077–40)

Naval women forming a Guard of Honour at HMS *Drake*, 1995
Women serving in the modern Royal Navy present a very different picture from their predecessors who served during the First and Second World Wars. The Service was disbanded in 1993, with total integration including compulsory sea service introduced by 1994. (Crown Copyright)

Wrens on board HMS *Brilliant*, 1990
Many changes have taken place in the years since 1990 when voluntary sea service was introduced but these Wrens using the large visual signal lamp on board HMS *Brilliant* would still be recognised by their Second World War counterparts. Not everything has changed! (Crown Copyright)

CHAPTER TWO
THE DOMESTIC BRANCH

Wren Cooks show off some of their kitchen equipment, *c.* 1941
The Cooks category was one of the first to be introduced and grew to be one of the largest, numbering many hundreds. These Cooks are with naval senior rates who oversaw the preparation of hundreds of meals every day. They were eventually replaced by WRNS senior rates. (RNM, 350/88 (170*39))

Wren Cooks and sailors, *c.* **1944**
Wren Cooks engaging in banter with sailors while delivering a hot meal to a field kitchen. It was not always possible for sailors to leave their posts and go to the galley for their meals so they were delivered to them instead! It also provided a welcome break for the Wrens from the heat and noise of the kitchens. (RNM, 24/91 (154))

Opposite: **Wren Cooks in the galley of a Fleet Air Arm station,** *c.* **1942**
Cooks like these were responsible for producing hundreds of meals every day with basic equipment and limited ingredients. Their working days could be very long and constantly busy, especially on FAA stations which operated twenty-four hours a day. (Courtesy of the Fleet Air Arm Museum, Crown Copyright)

A group of Cooks and Stewards taking a breather, *c.* 1944
Naval galleys were hot, cramped, very noisy and a constant hive of activity, so a breath of fresh air and some exercise would be very welcome indeed! (RNM, 350/88 (170*37))

Opposite, above: **Wardroom staff of HMS *Daedalus*, 1942**
WRNS Stewards were responsible for looking after the accommodation of both WRNS and naval personnel and the category, introduced in the summer of 1940, also included Laundrymaids, Cleaners and Kitchenmaids. It grew into one of the largest and most widespread categories and many of its Wrens served overseas as well. (RNM, 182/89 (4))

Below: **WRNS Stewards tidying the entrance to quarters, *c.* 1942**
The tasks that were required of them were sometimes physical and demanding, and Stewards needed to be strong and adaptable. (RNM, 350/88 (170*27))

Chapter Three
The Clerical and Supply Branches

A WRNS regulating office, *c.* 1942
The rapid expansion of the WRNS led to a huge increase in the number of WRNS personnel engaged on administrative work. One of the larger clerical categories was the Regulating ratings who were mainly responsible for maintaining discipline. Here a Petty Officer is keeping her Unit Officer up to date. (Lee Miller Archive, 5786–89)

Cleaning a glazing machine, *c.* **1942**
One of the jobs of the Wren Writers was to assist in the production of photographic prints. This Wren is polishing the drum of a Velox glazing machine, used to produce a glossy finish on bromide prints. (Lee Miller Archive, 5786–97)

WRNS personnel in a fleet mail office, *c.* 1943
These Wrens are working in a large fleet mail office, one of the busiest and most important places on a naval establishment. The regular supply of mail was vital for morale, especially for sailors on board ships. (Lee Miller Archive, 5208–130)

A Quarters Officer and Assistant, HMS *Seahawk*, c. 1943
The Supply category also included personnel responsible for the supply of victuals to galleys. This work was eventually done entirely by Wrens. (RNM, 350/88 (126*5))

A Wren Supply Assistant issuing sailors with amenities, *c.* 1943
The WRNS Supply Branch was very large and included a wide variety of jobs. The category continually grew and changed as the Service expanded and most stores depots, like this one supplying sailors from trawlers, were run entirely by WRNS personnel. (Lee Miller Archive, 5208–8)

The staff of the Dependants Allowance Office, Portsmouth, 1944
Late in 1943 a separate category of Writers (Pay) (RM) was introduced and these Wrens can be seen wearing the Royal Marines cap badge. They were trained especially to work with the Royal Marines and even trained separately from other Wren Writers. They were very proud of the distinction. (RNM, 387/89 (2))

A very unusual occurrence, *c.* 1943
Rum was never officially issued to Wrens but on certain important occasions they could, with their Unit Officer's permission, take part in 'splicing the mainbrace'. These happy Wrens at RNAS Yeovilton are queuing to receive their ration from their Supply Wren colleagues. (Courtesy of the Fleet Air Arm Museum)

The staff of the British Fleet Mail Office, Reading, 1944
Fleet mail offices were extremely important and busy places and many hundreds of WRNS Clerical ratings and Administrative Officers were employed in them. The Reading office was obviously a particularly busy place! (RNM, 339/90 (26))

A very important job, *c.* **1942**
The issue of rum was a vital part of naval daily routine and tradition which was not allowed to be disrupted by wartime conditions. These Wren Supply Assistants are in charge of the issue from the victualling shed of a large south coast establishment. (Lee Miller Archive, 5208–51)

The most popular Supply Wren, *c.* **1943!**
WRNS ratings could buy additional 'goodies' from small shops staffed by Supply Assistants. This happy group have probably just been paid and are stocking up on the essentials! They are joined by a Canadian woman from the WRCNS, which was created in 1942 after three very senior WRNS officers went to Canada to set it up. In 1943 a number of Canadian personnel came to the UK to serve in London and Scotland. (Lee Miller Archive, 5763–3)

CHAPTER 4
THE TECHNICAL TRADES

Above and opposite: **Wren Torpedomen working on the firing mechanism of a depth-charge, *c.* 1942**
The Wren Torpedoman category was introduced in the summer of 1942 after a serious shortage of naval ratings caused problems with maintenance of torpedoes and depth-charges. The Wrens carried out exactly the same work as their male counterparts in what was a vitally important role; many of them were employed by Coastal Forces. (Lee Miller Archive, 5077–34; 5786–83)

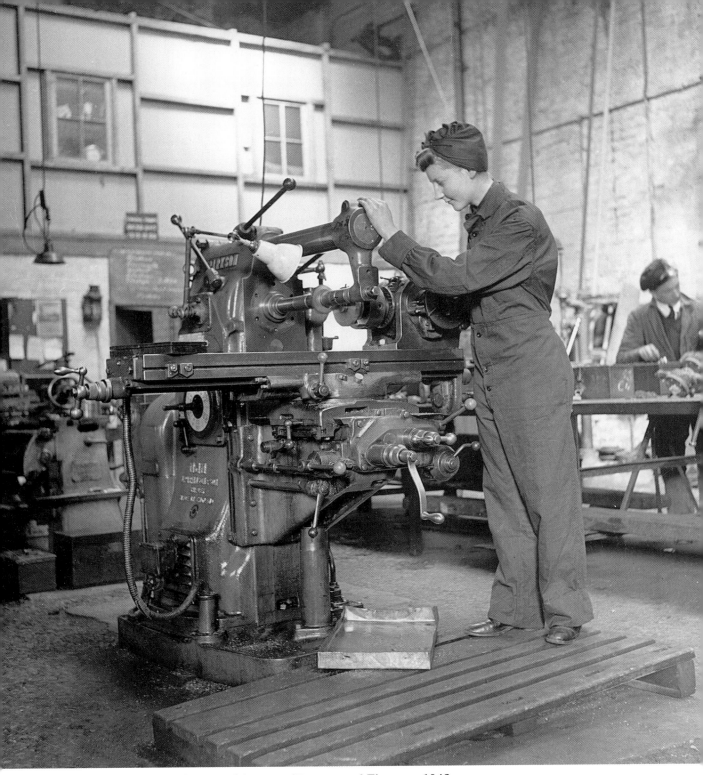

A Qualified Ordnance Wren working as a Turner and Fitter, *c.* **1943**
The Qualified Ordnance category, which was created in September 1941, was one of the most technical of categories. The Wrens were responsible for the maintenance of ship and aircraft small guns. This work included, among other things, fitting and turning, crane and tractor driving, carpentry, sail-making and electrical maintenance. (Lee Miller Archive, 5077–126)

Torpedo Wrens in the torpedo workshop at Fort Blockhouse, Gosport, 1943
(Courtesy of the Royal Navy Submarine Museum)

Torpedo Wrens attaching firing mechanisms to magnetic and acoustic mines, HMS *Vernon*, c. 1942
(RNM, 40/88 (7))

Meteorological Wrens taking readings, *c.* **1941**
(Lee Miller Archive, 5786–36)

Meteorological Wrens at HMS *Kestrel*, Worthy Down, 1943
This category was introduced in the summer of 1941 with the Wrens working on Fleet Air Arm stations. Their work involved making weather observations, watching cloud type and movements, recording temperatures and noting wind speeds and direction. They also checked visibility and the information they collected was vitally important for judging flying conditions for the FAA pilots. (RNM, 350/88 (171*3))

A WRNS officer working as a Submarine Attack Teacher, HMS *Dolphin*, c. 1943
This was a small but very significant category. Submarine Attack Teachers were originally Torpedo Wrens who were specifically trained to help submarine commanders learn their submarine warfare tactics. They worked on movement tables and training equipment, and several officers went on to become instructors and were entirely responsible for naval officer training and for assessing their abilities when they received new or refresher training. (Courtesy of the Royal Navy Submarine Museum)

The Duchess of Kent visits Granton Naval Base, 1942
Princess Marina, Duchess of Kent, was Chief Commandant of the WRNS and visited as many WRNS units as possible. She was always keen to see Wrens at work and on her visit to Granton a Qualified Ordnance Wren explained the intricacies of a firing mechanism. (RNM, 5/76 (20))

An Aircraft Direction Wren at her plotting table, HMS *Urley*, Isle of Man, 1944
These Wrens were responsible for plotting the movements of both naval and enemy aircraft once the use of radar had become widespread. The information was passed on to those responsible for carrying out operational planning. The category was later merged with other air-related categories and became the Radar Plotter category in 1949. (Courtesy of the Fleet Air Arm Museum)

Opposite: **Qualified Ordnance Wrens stripping down aircraft guns, *c.* 1944**
Two qualified Ordnance Wrens strip, clean and reassemble aircraft weapons. They had to be able to identify and maintain the smallest components of all the various guns used on naval aircraft. Their work was vitally important as aircrews were entirely reliant on their weaponry for both attack and defence. (Lee Miller Archive, 5842–79)

Trainee Air Mechanic Class L7 at HMS *Fledgling*, Mill Meece, Staffordshire, *c.* 1943

HMS *Fledgling* was unique. It was the only training school created exclusively for Wrens. Air Mechanic classes passed through at regular intervals and on completion of their training, which could last between eighteen and twenty-one weeks at *Fledgling* depending on their specialisation, they invariably went straight to work on naval air stations. In many cases the Wrens were solely responsible for maintaining aircraft airframes, engines, ordnance or electrics. (RNM, 434/87 (20))

A Cinema Operator with her projector, 1942

The Cinema Operator category was introduced in July 1941 with the Wrens being trained by the Gaumont Picture Corporation. They had to know exactly how to operate and maintain the projectors and most of their work involved showing instructional or training films. (Lee Miller Archive, 4998–14)

Wren Air Mechanics (Radio) maintaining aircraft radio equipment, *c.* **1942**
These Wrens were trained specifically to fit and maintain the radio equipment in naval aircraft. The equipment was checked after every flight and quite often the mechanics would fly with the aircraft to check ground/air communications. If there was a problem it could be dealt with immediately. (Courtesy of the Fleet Air Arm Museum, Crown Copyright)

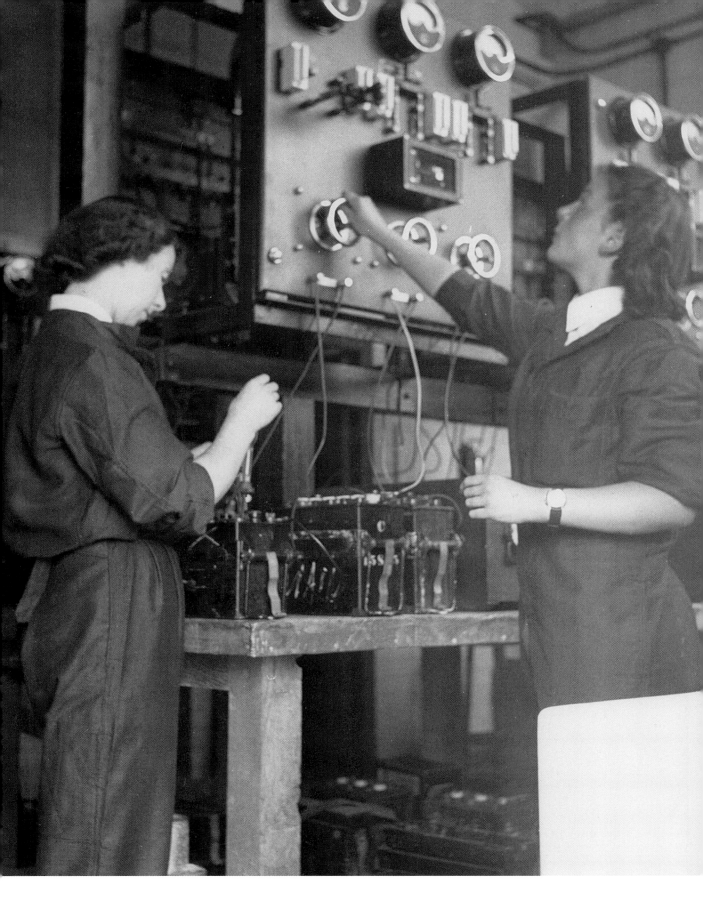

Boats Crew Wrens with a twin Lewis gun, *c.* **1943**
Although not strictly regarded as a Technical category, Boats Crew Wrens still had to learn other skills besides those of their trade. Not only were they responsible for the use and maintenance of the boats in their charge but they were also expected to protect them if necessary. Some of the larger boats operating in areas vulnerable to air attack were fitted with twin Lewis guns. (RNM, 119/1993 (4))

Opposite: **Battery Chargers maintaining aircraft batteries,** *c.* **1942**
The Battery Chargers were one of the smallest categories. The Wrens invariably worked on small outlying air stations and their job was to remove and recharge the batteries of aircraft returning from operations. Not only did the Wrens have to be physically strong and endure long periods of inactivity but the work was regarded as highly dangerous because of exposure to chemicals and acids, which were believed to be harmful to their fertility. (Lee Miller Archive, 4078–134)

CHAPTER FIVE
THE COMMUNICATIONS BRANCH

Visual Signaller Wrens signalling to ships of the Allied invasion force, June 1944
(RNM, 350/88 (170*33))

A Leading Wren Visual Signaller, *c.* **1944**
The Visual Signaller category was introduced in October 1942 with the Wrens being trained in all signalling methods including signal projectors, Aldis lamps and flags. (Lee Miller Archive, 5790–33)

Visual Signaller Wrens, *c*. 1943
Visual Signaller Wrens are using an Aldis lamp to announce the arrival of a WRNS Boarding Officer, seen here in the wheelhouse of the ship. (Lee Miller Archive, 5645–79)

Visual Signaller Wrens communicating with signal flags, *c.* **1943**
(Lee Miller Archive, 5077–10)

The Visual Signaller Wrens of Dunoon Pilot Station, 1945
(RNM, 24/91 (174))

WRNS and naval personnel in one of the planning offices in the tunnels below Fort Southwick during D-Day operations, June 1944
(Courtesy of *Portsmouth News*)

Opposite, above: **The first class of Visual Signaller Wrens to qualify at HMS *Cabbala*, February 1943**
(Courtesy of the Fleet Air Arm Museum)

Below: **Wireless Telegraphy Operators in the tunnels below Fort Southwick, Portsmouth, during D-Day operations, June 1944**
Much of the operational organisation for D-Day was conducted in the tunnels below the Fort, with most communications work being carried out by WRNS personnel. Their work was vitally important as many thousands of signals were sent and received during the few days before and on D-Day itself. The signal traffic was even heavier as Operation Neptune, the naval element of D-Day, was enormous and each vessel needed to remain in touch to receive orders and relay positions. All this was carried out under extreme pressure, with the utmost secrecy and in working conditions that were far from ideal. (Courtesy of *Portsmouth News*)

WRNS Routeing Officer and Plotter in a naval shipping movements office, *c.* **1943**

(Courtesy of *Portsmouth News*)

Two Wireless Telegraphy Wrens keep in touch with local shipping, *c*. 1942
Wireless Telegraphy was one of a number of Communications categories that were created in 1940 or 1941, all of which required specialist training. Eventually, Wrens replaced just about every sailor and naval officer working in communications and it became the biggest of all the branches. (Lee Miller Archive, 5790–27)

A Wireless Telegraphist using radio to talk to a pilot on a test flight, *c.* **1943**
(Lee Miller Archive, 5790–38)

Opposite, above: **Chief Wrens at Scarborough, 1940**
This group was the first to train as Special Wireless Telegraphy Operators. They were trained at HMS *Flowerdown* near Scarborough and on completion they were rated as Chief Wrens. Most of this group were among the first overseas draft which left for Singapore in January 1941. (RNM, 97/87 (14))

Below: **A Radio Telegraphy Operator Wren working at Speckington Manor, Yeovilton, January 1943**
By the end of 1940 the first Wren R/T Operators had completed their six months of training and were sent to work mainly at various VHF stations. (Courtesy of the Fleet Air Arm Museum)

A group of mixed category Communications Wrens at HMS *Sparrowhawk*, Hatston, in the Orkney Islands, 1944
Many units had large numbers of Communications Wrens, especially on outlying stations, which were responsible for monitoring communications traffic. This work involved different types of expertise, hence the variety of categories that could be found on any one station. (RNM, 24/91 (135*3))

Opposite: **A group of Radio Telegraphy Operators undergoing training, *c.* 1941**
The training for R/T Wrens was long and very comprehensive and Wren Operators were highly regarded for their efficiency and coolness under pressure. They were thought to be better suited for the work than many of the sailors they replaced. (Courtesy of the Fleet Air Arm Museum, Crown Copyright)

CHAPTER SIX
THE FLEET AIR ARM

The plotting room in the control tower at HMS _Urley_, RNAS Ronaldsway, Isle of Man, _c._ 1943
Many Wrens worked with the Naval Air Control Service on naval air stations monitoring the movements of naval aircraft during flying missions and training exercises. (Courtesy of the Fleet Air Arm Museum)

A group of Aircraft Mechanics, *c.* 1943
Aircraft Mechanics were responsible for the repair and maintenance of Fleet Air Arm aircraft, a highly important part of the war effort. Pilots relied on the Wren Mechanics to keep their aircraft operational. (Lee Miller Archive, 5790–21)

A class of trainee Air Mechanics at HMS _Fledgling_, Mill Meece, Staffordshire, August 1943
HMS _Fledgling_ was the only training establishment opened for Wrens and trainee Air Mechanics would spend between six and fourteen weeks here learning their trade before being sent almost exclusively to naval air stations. (RNM, 24/91 (159))

An Air Mechanic (Radio) in the cockpit of an aircraft, *c.* 1941
It was vitally important for pilots to be able to maintain radio contact with both their fellow pilots and with their operational headquarters. Air mechanics (R) were responsible for repairing and maintaining the radio equipment in the aircraft and occasionally flew with them to check that it was working properly. (Courtesy of the Fleet Air Arm Museum, Crown Copyright)

Air Fighter Control Wrens at the Training School for Fighter Pilots, RNAS Yeovilton, 1941
This strange-looking activity was designed to monitor the accuracy of bombing by fighter pilots undergoing training. (Courtesy of the Fleet Air Arm Museum)

A Wren Photographer with her aerial camera, 1942
Wren Photographers were introduced in November 1941 to take and process photographs on naval air stations. They assisted other categories that required photographic support and also helped train FAA personnel in aircraft recognition. For some it was part of their normal duties to fly in aircraft and take aerial photographs which could later be used by Naval Intelligence. (Courtesy of the Fleet Air Arm Museum, Crown Copyright)

A unusual breed of Wren, 1941
This WRNS fire-fighting team at RNAS St Merryn, Cornwall, consisted of a combination of Wrens from different FAA categories who could be called upon to help if there was an emergency on the airfield. (Courtesy of the Fleet Air Arm Museum)

CHAPTER SEVEN
INFINITE VARIETY

Education Wrens in a mobile household van, *c.* 1947
When the run-down of the Service began late in 1944, there was a need to help prepare Wrens for their reintroduction into civilian life. The WRNS equipped three mobile household vans which travelled around the country visiting WRNS units. They were operated by Education Wrens who taught such things as housecraft and dressmaking. (RNM, 24/91 (165))

Fleet Mail Wrens delivering mail to ships by boat, *c.* **1943**
This category was introduced in 1942 as part of the Naval Censorship Branch. Once the mail had been checked it could be delivered to the eagerly waiting sailors on board their ships. It was extremely important for maintaining morale that the mail was delivered regularly. (Lee Miller Archive, 5262–30)

A Parachute Packer checking parachutes for damage, *c*. 1942
The Parachute Packer category was introduced in the summer of 1940 with the Wrens working mainly on naval air stations. They needed to be not only physically strong but also meticulous as the slightest mistake in checking for stitching errors or tears in the fabric or in the packing itself could lead to disaster for the user of the parachute. It was a highly responsible job. (Lee Miller Archive, 4078–143)

A Boarding Officer shows her agility, *c.* **1943**
Working with the Naval Control Service, Boarding Officers, who began their work in 1943, were responsible for delivering and explaining confidential orders to ships' captains. If the ships were leaving port they frequently had to stay on board until the ship returned, sometimes weeks later. Boarding officers were among the few WRNS personnel to do this as part of their regular duties. (Lee Miller Archive, 5645–71)

Boarding Officers in action, _c._ 1942
Boarding Officers had to be young and very fit because after an eight-week training course they would be expected to be able to board any size of merchant ship in any kind of weather. (RNM, 24/91 (157); RNM, 24/91 (175))

Maintenance Wrens carry out repair work on a Coastal Forces boat, *c.* **1943**
Maintenance category Wrens began to appear in increasingly large numbers in 1941 owing to the rapid expansion of Coastal Forces. Their duties were very varied and many of the Wrens worked to repair and maintain the fast craft used by Coastal Forces, and it was not unknown for them to return a badly damaged boat back to action in less than forty-eight hours. The variety of work of the Maintenance Wrens led to the creation of a number of other specialised categories as demand grew. (Lee Miller Archive, 5842–75)

A Maintenance Wren and her tractor, *c.* 1943
The work of the Maintenance Wrens was very varied and it was not unusual to see such sights as a Wren driving a very large tractor to tow a Coastal Forces boat out of a repair shed. (Lee Miller Archive, 5208–139)

A Wren M/T Driver and her vehicle, *c.* **1943**
Motor Transport Driver was one of the earliest categories created and, although only experienced drivers were recruited at first, it quickly became obvious that demand was going to outstrip supply. By April 1944 a loan of WAAF drivers was needed but eventually WRNS training schools were opened in London and Liverpool. As the war progressed, the size of vehicle the Wrens were allowed to drive increased until some were in charge of 10-ton trucks. (Lee Miller Archive, 5786–86)

The Wrens of HMS *Northney*, Hayling Island, October 1944

HMS *Northney* on Hayling Island, near Portsmouth, was one of many Combined Operations Bases spread along the south coast. Because of the nature of the work on the base, most of the Wrens in this photograph were either Clerical, Technical or Domestic workers. This combination was typical of the varied work carried out by Wrens on many naval bases. It was also compulsory to have a VAD nurse wherever Wrens were serving so she could take care of female health problems. (RNM, 278/89 (2))

WRNS Gardeners at Woodstock House near Portsmouth, *c.* 1944

Woodstock House was one of a number of WRNS quarters situated near Fort Southwick, the D-Day operational headquarters. The Gardener category was introduced early in 1944 to help maintain the grounds of the properties requisitioned by the Royal Navy. These included large private estates and schools. The gardeners were required to have had college-based horticultural training and so were classified as a 'specialised' category. In their off-duty time they helped tend the vegetable gardens and produced extra provisions for the Wrens occupying the house. (Loaned by Mrs K. Adams)

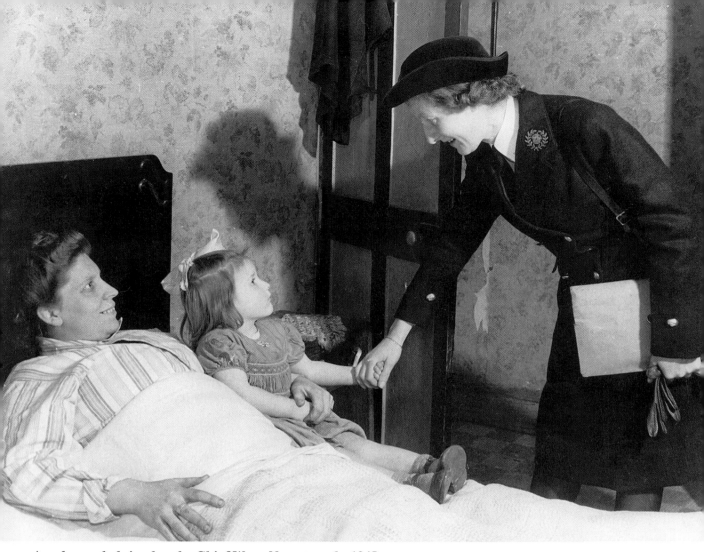

A welcome helping hand – Chief Wren Nye at work, 1945
The Welfare Worker category evolved from the Administrative category, which was renamed the Regulating category in May 1945. Previously some WRNS senior rates had been temporarily seconded to help naval Welfare Officers with an increasingly heavy workload. They formed the basis for the new Welfare Worker category which was created with fifty specially trained Chief Wrens. They were mainly involved in looking after or helping naval wives in times of difficulty and were seen as invaluable to naval morale. (Courtesy of the Royal Navy Submarine Museum, Crown Copyright)

WRNS inspection at the Royal Naval Barracks, Chatham, 1942

Although Wrens had been working with the Royal Marines since quite early on in the war, it was decided in 1943 that those Wrens who had been employed on pay and secretarial duties should form a separate specialised category of Writer (RM). These Wrens were unique because they were allowed to wear the Royal Marines cap badge instead of the usual cap tally. They were extremely proud of this distinction and competition to join the category was stiff. (RNM, 239/88 (5))

First Officer Esta Eldod, WRNS Press Officer, c. 1942

First Officer Eldod was appointed as the first WRNS Press Officer in the autumn of 1940. Already an experienced journalist, her role was to liaise with the press and organise recruiting publicity. She was responsible for co-ordinating the photography done by Lee Miller and accompanied her as she toured south coast establishments taking pictures of Wrens at work. (RNM, 350/88 (96*19))

Above and left: **The Admiralty Despatch Riders, *c.* 1940**

The Despatch Rider category was one of the first to be created. They were already employed at the Admiralty by the end of 1939 and by the spring of 1940 had completely replaced male riders. By the end of 1940 category numbers had increased dramatically although those recruited had to be experienced motorcycle riders, which initially limited the number of women who could join. Their work was hard and dangerous, particularly in London during the Blitz, but all riders faced many hazards. They were continually praised for their skill, determination and bravery. (RNM, 24/91 (158); RNM, 350/88 (27*7))

Opposite: **A unique Wren, *c.* 1942**

Leading Wren Margaret Young was the only WRNS blacksmith and she worked in the submarine workshop at Fort Blockhouse in Gosport. There was no official category for blacksmiths and Leading Wren Young was probably a Maintenance or Torpedo Wren whose special talent was put to good use. (RNM, 24/91 (163))

A Wren Welder in action, 1943
Yet another of the skills acquired by Maintenance Wrens. Some Wrens specialised in welding as part of their maintenance and repair work. (Lee Miller Archive, 4998–46)

DEMS Wrens ready to go to work, *c.* **1943**
A number of merchant ships were converted to carry weapons for protection on convoys. These Defensively Equipped Merchant Ships (DEMS) also needed help with communications and so in early 1943 a new DEMS category was created. Most of the ratings were Coders and most of the officers were Cypher Officers. They boarded ships to test equipment and train the crews in the use of some of the radio equipment. Eventually two officers were trained as Armaments Inspectors and carried out regular checks on the weaponry. This was one of the few categories where Wrens could spend time at sea while carrying out their duties. (Lee Miller Archive, 5645–69)

The Boats Crew Wrens – a Jenny of All Trades, *c.* **1943**
The work of Boats Crew Wrens was very varied, as can be seen from this and the following four photographs, which all date from about 1943. While primarily responsible for the maintenance and operation of small boats, they were also expected to be able to board all boats under any conditions, to be navigators and pilots, and to do all their own repair work, whether it involved engines or ropework. Within the category, Wrens could also become Boat Drivers or Stokers – highly sought-after duties. The work could be filthy, tiring and in some cases very dangerous but competition to join the category was fierce as Boats Crew Wrens regarded themselves as a special breed of Wren. (Lee Miller Archive, 5842–85)

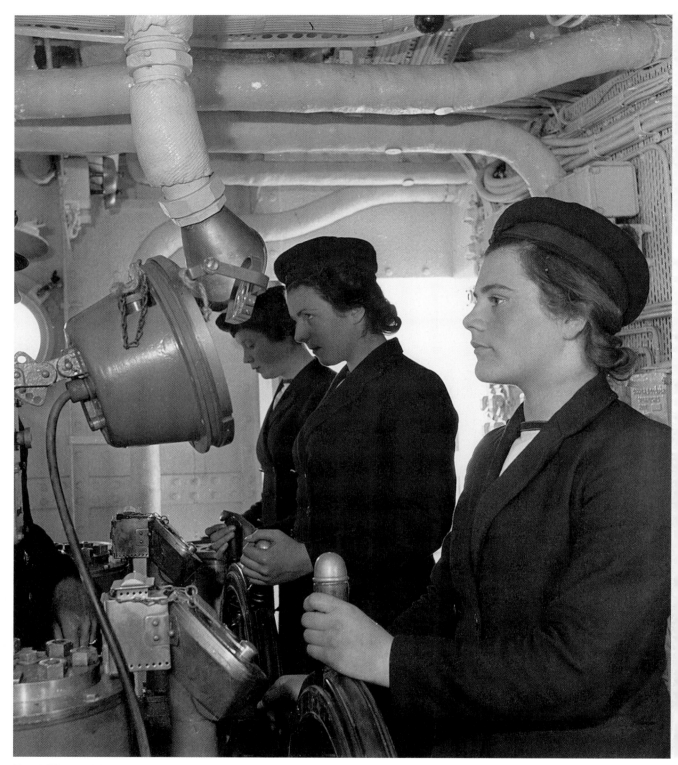

(Lee Miller Archive, 5077–159)

(Lee Miller Archive, 5077–164)

(RNM, 350/88 (170*31))

Chapter Eight
OVERSEAS

The ill-fated SS *Aguila*, c. 1941
The SS *Aguila* was carrying the first draft of twenty-two WRNS personnel and a Nursing Sister to Gibraltar. As part of Convoy OG 71 the *Aguila* left Liverpool on 12 August 1941 but was sunk seven days later. The specially chosen Wrens – 12 Cypher Officers and 10 Chief Wren Special Operators – and the Nursing Sister all perished. This emphasised the danger of travelling in merchant ships, a policy that was changed after the loss of the *Aguila* and other ships carrying Wrens and thereafter all other WRNS personnel drafted overseas were transported on naval ships or troopships. (RNM, 24/91 (120*55))

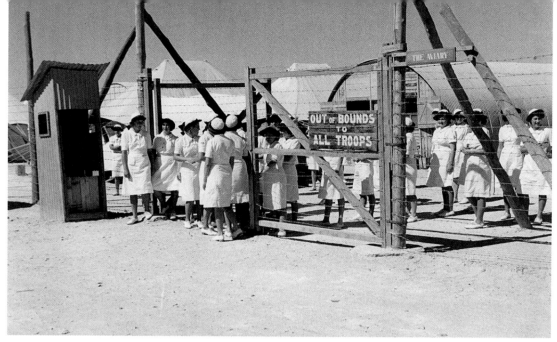

'The Aviary' on the desert road to Cairo, c. 1942–3

For many Wrens drafted overseas it was their first experience of a very different way of life. For some lucky Wrens the accommodation could be quite luxurious but many others found themselves in much more basic living quarters. (RNM, 102/88 (5))

The first overseas draft, January 1941

The first overseas draft left England for Singapore in January 1941. It consisted of twenty specially chosen and trained Chief Wren Special Wireless Telegraphy Operators, Second Officer Betty Archdale, who was the Officer-in-Charge, and a naval Nursing Sister. In February 1942 they were very hurriedly evacuated to Ceylon just before the fall of Singapore. (RNM, 24/91 (134*2))

Safely in Ceylon, February 1942
Just before the fall of Singapore in February 1942, the first overseas draft was evacuated to Ceylon and sent to Colombo to continue their specialist work of monitoring Japanese radio traffic. (RNM, 24/91 (134*3))

WRNS Officers at Cape Town, South Africa, February 1945
Early in 1945 there had been a large number of Wrens serving at HMS *Gnu* in Cape Town but by August of that year the number of officers had been reduced to just five. Most other officers and ratings had been drafted back to the UK to be demobilised. (RNM, 94/88 (11))

Into Europe, 1944
In August 1944 the first contingent of Wrens to land on mainland Europe arrived by landing craft at Arromanches in Normandy. They were mainly Cooks and Stewards who were very shortly followed by Writers and Communications Wrens who were to join the staff of Admiral Ramsay, Allied Naval Commander Expeditionary Force (ANCXF) in Normandy. They then followed the Allied advance into Europe. (RNM, 239/88 (8))

The desert Wrens, Alexandria, 1942
The WRNS unit at HMS *Nile* was one of the largest outside the UK. This photograph, taken outside their quarters in the Convent of Notre Dame in Alexandria on the day they arrived early in 1942, shows the large numbers of Wrens that were drafted to some overseas establishments. In the summer of 1942 they were all evacuated to Ismailia for their own safety and thence moved on to other stations. (RNM, 102/88 (7))

WRNS quarters in Singapore, 1941

The rather luxurious quarters at Kranji Wireless Telegraphy Station were home to the first draft of Wrens sent to Singapore in January 1941. Although life in Singapore was uncomfortable for women more used to the cleanliness and temperate climate of England, the quarters were specially built to provide some comfort. Their sojourn here was short-lived as they were soon evacuated to Ceylon in advance of the fall of Singapore. (RNM, 24/91 (134*8))

New sights and other luxuries, South Africa, 1942

Many Wrens were experiencing life overseas for the first time and although their work was vitally important they still found time to enjoy some of the luxuries that were not available at home because of rationing. These off-duty Wrens from HMS *Kongoni* in Durban are making the most of their new experiences. (RNM, 97/88 (14))

CHAPTER NINE
CONCLUSION

The WRNS unit at the Royal Marines Barracks, Eastney, Portsmouth, 1956
The reduction in numbers of Wrens began in 1944 but continued into the next decade as the Service redefined its post-war role. By the mid-1950s even the largest naval establishments had only small numbers of WRNS personnel. (RNM, 350/88 (134*2))

Above and opposite: **A time for relaxation, *c.* 1943**
Despite the tremendous hard work and endeavour of all members of the WRNS during the Second World War, they still managed to find some precious moments for relaxation. The methods may have been different between officers and ratings but the desired effect was the same – to enjoy the company of comrades and to recharge the batteries for a few hours.
(RNM, 350/88 (96*6); RNM, 69/91)

The modern pioneers, 1990

This was the first group of Wrens to volunteer for sea service. On 8 October 1990 they joined HMS *Brilliant*, the first Royal Navy ship ever to carry women as part of the crew. (Crown Copyright)

Right: **Another first, *c.* 1994**
Although some Wrens had been taught to shoot during the Second World War, the early 1990s saw the introduction of training in the use of weapons for security and ceremonial purposes. These Wrens at HMS *Daedalus* look very confident as they prepare to form part of a Guard of Honour. (Crown Copyright)

Opposite: **Change is coming, *c.* 1978**
The late 1970s saw a major change when the WRNS became subject to the Naval Discipline Act in 1977. This was the first sign of equality with their male counterparts but Wrens carried on as normal. At the School of Maritime Operations, HMS *Dryad*, a Wren (Radar) instructs a naval officer in the use of radar equipment. (RNM, 24/91 (120*27))

Above: **Some things never change, June 2000**
This Wren on board HMS *Cornwall* in June 2000 would probably be recognisable to a Second World War Maintenance Wren. Some of the work done on board ship hasn't changed much and naval women are involved in the day-to-day maintenance of the ships. (Crown Copyright)

Opposite: **Hot work! A fire-fighting exercise, 2000**
For many years one of the arguments against Wrens serving on board warships was that they would not be strong enough to carry out the same tasks as the men. This has proved true in some cases but most women serving on ships have shown they are as capable as their male colleagues of carrying out heavy-duty tasks. (Crown Copyright)

It's only the setting that's different, c. 1998

This cook may be working in the ship's galley deep below decks on board HMS *Cornwall* but someone still has to peel the carrots ready to feed the ship's company – a job her Second World War counterpart would have done! (Crown Copyright)

Radar Operators on HMS *Brilliant*, 1991

Once again the setting is different, and the equipment far more sophisticated but a radar Wren from the 1940s would probably recognise at least some of what her 'descendants' are doing and possibly envy them just a little! (Crown Copyright)

CHAPTER TEN
STATISTICS

Shortly after the outbreak of the Second World War in September 1939 the Women's Royal Naval Service began to grow to a size – and at a speed – no one had foreseen. The initial view of the Admiralty was that a Service equivalent in size to that anticipated for the First World War, approximately 3,000 women, would be sufficient. The following lists illustrate the growth and spread of the WRNS during the Second World War in comparison to the Service during the First World War and in more recent years.

Just as the number of women serving far exceeded all expectations, so the diversity of work undertaken rapidly outgrew official thinking. The WRNS became an integral yet almost self-sufficient part of the Royal Navy which proved vital to the overall operational success of the Senior Service.

Places Served in the UK

First World War

WRNS Headquarters
Crystal Palace Training Depot

Divisions:

Bristol
Chatham
Harwich
Irish
Liverpool

London
Portsmouth Subdivision
Scotland
South West
Tynemouth

HM Ships:

Apollo
Crescent
Island Prince
Powerful

There were over seventy-five different locations in total within Divisions.

Shore Establishments:

Abatos	*Daedalus*	*Godwit*	*Mersey*
Aggressive	*Dartmouth*	*Goldcrest*	*Midge*
Allenby	*Defender*	*Gosling*	*Minos*
Ambrose	*Demetrius*		*Monck*
Appledore	*Dinosaur*	*Haig*	*Mylodon*
Arbella	*Dinosaur II*	*Helder*	
Ariel	*Dipper*	*Helicon*	*Nemo*
Armadillo	*Dolphin*	*Heron*	*Newt*
Attack	*Dragonfly*	*Hornbill*	*Nighthawk*
	Drake	*Hornet*	*Nightjar*
Bacchante	*Dryad*		*Nimrod*
Badger	*Duke*	*Impregnable*	*Northney*
Beaverk	*Dundonald*	*Irwell*	*Nuthatch*
Beaver II	*Dundonald II*		
Bee		*Jackdaw*	*Odyssey*
Beehive	*Eaglet*	*James Cook*	*Orlando*
Black Bat	*Elfin*		*Osborne*
Blackcap	*Europa*	*Kestrel*	*Osprey*
Boscawen	*Excalibur*	*King Alfred*	*Owl*
Britannia	*Excellent*		
Brontosaurus		*Landrail*	*Paragon*
Bruce	*Faraway*	*Leigh*	*Pasco*
Bunting	*Ferret*	*Lizard*	*Peewit*
	Fervent	*Lochailort*	*Pembroke I–V*
Cabbala	*Fieldfare*	*Lochinvar*	*Pomona*
Cabot	*Fledgling*	*Louisberg*	*Porcupine*
Caledonia	*Flora*	*Lucifer*	*President*
Calliope	*Flowerdown*	*Lynx*	*Prosperine*
Caroline	*Foliot*		*Pyramus*
Cicala	*Foliot II*	*Macaw*	
Claverhouse	*Forte*	*Manatee*	*Quebec*
Clio	*Fortitude*	*Mantis*	*Queen Charlotte*
Cochrane	*Forward*	*Marlborough*	
Collingwood	*Fox*	*Martello*	*Racer I*
Condor		*Mastodon*	*Racer II*
Copra	*Gadwall*	*Medina*	*Raleigh*
Cressy	*Ganges*	*Mentor*	*Raven*
Cricket	*Gannet*	*Mercury*	*Revlis*
Curlew	*Glendower*	*Mercury II*	*Ringtail I*
	Glenholt	*Merlin*	*Ringtail II*

Robertson	*Scotia*	*Tern*	*Vectis*
Robin	*Seahawk*	*Torch I*	*Vernon*
Rooke	*Sea Serpent*	*Torch II*	*Victory I–V*
Rosneath	*Shrapnel*	*Tormentor*	*Volcano*
Royal Arthur	*Shrike*	*Trelawney*	*Vulture*
	Skirmisher I	*Turtle*	
St Andrew	*Skirmisher II*		*Warren*
St Barbara	*Sparrowhawk*	*Ubiquity*	*Wasp*
St Christopher	*Spartiate I*	*Unicorn*	*Watchful*
St Clement	*Spartiate II*	*Urley*	*Waxwing*
St Columbia	*Squid*		*Wellesley*
St George	*Stopford*	*Valkyrie I*	*Westcliff*
St Matthew		*Valkyrie II*	*Western Isles*
St Vincent	*Tadpole*	*Varbel I*	*Wildfire*
Sanderling	*Tennyson*	*Varbel II*	*Woolverstone*

RN Barracks Chatham
RM Barracks Chatham
RN Barracks Plymouth
RN Barracks Portsmouth
WRNS Headquarters
Royal Naval College, Greenwich
Free French Ships: *Marshal Soult*; *Marshal Ney*; *Paris*

Post-1986

Shore Establishments:

BRNC, Dartmouth	*Mercury**
Caledonia	MOD London
Cambridge	*Nelson*
*Centurion**	*Neptune*
*Cochrane**	*Osprey**
Collingwood	*President**
*Daedalus**	*Raleigh*
Dolphin	*Royal Arthur**
Drake	*St Vincent**
Dryad	*Seahawk*
Excellent	*Sultan*
*Fisgard**	*Temeraire*
Forest Moor	*Vernon**
Gannet	*Victory*
Heron	*Warrior* (name changed to *JSU Northwood*)
*RNC, Greenwich**	

Colchester Military Detention Centre
HM Naval Base, Plymouth
HM Naval Base, Portsmouth
Royal Hospital, Haslar
Royal Marines School of Music
Various RAF Stations

* Establishments marked with an asterisk have undergone name changes or have closed down in recent years.

Overseas Service

First World War

Genoa
Gibraltar
Malta

To End of 1945

South Africa:	**Australia:**	**Europe:**
Afrikander	*Cerebus*	Naval Parties France
Assegai	*Golden Hind*	Naval Parties Germany
Gnu	*RNH Herne Bay*	
Hopetown	*Rushcutter*	
Kongoni		
Korongo (Kenya)		
Malagas		
Tane (East Africa)		

North Africa/Mediterranean:	**India/Ceylon:**	**USA:**
Byrsa	*Anderson*	*Saker*
Cormorant	*Bambara*	Also Baltimore
Euphrates	*Bherunda*	Long Island
Grebe	*Braganza*	New York
Hannibal	*Garuda*	Philadelphia
Medway II	*Hathi*	San Francisco
Moreta	*Highflyer*	San Pedro
Nile	*Lanka*	Tampa
Osiris	*Ukassa*	
Phoenix	*Ursa*	
St Angelo	*Vallura*	
Sheba		
Stag		

Post-war to Present

Belgium
Canada
Diego Garcia
Falkland Islands
Gibraltar
Hong Kong
Lisbon
Malta

Mauritius
Naples
Northern Ireland
Norway
Peking
Rhode Island, USA
Washington DC

Numbers

First World War

Total: 7,000
(Anticipated number 3,000)

Second World War

(Anticipated number 3,000)	
September 1939	1,601
End January 1941	10,653
End January 1942	22,898
End January 1943	41,415
End January 1944	66,500
June 1944	74,620
August 1945	63,395
December 1945	48,866

Post-war

June 1946	15,000
January 1948	7,000
September 1953	4,215
July 1966	3,260
August 1974	4,695
July 1980	c. 3,000
July 1990	c. 3,900
November 2001	3,436

Women in the Royal Navy, 2001

Number: 3,436

Serving at Sea:	904
Officers:	136
Ratings:	768

52 ships have female crew members (see below)
22 ships have officers and ratings
16 ships have officers only
  3 ships have ratings only

86 per cent of all female ratings are eligible for sea service.

HM Ships with Female Personnel in November 2001:

Albion
Alderney
Anglesey
Argyll
Ark Royal

Bangor
Beagle
Blyth
Bridport
Bulwark

Campbeltown
Cardiff
Chatham
Cornwall
Coventry
Cumberland

Dumbarton Castle

Echo
Edinburgh
Endurance
Enterprise
Exeter

Explorer

Fearless

Glasgow
Gloucester
Grafton
Grimsby
Guernsey

Illustrious
Invincible

Kent

Lancaster
Leeds Castle
Lindisfarne
Liverpool

Manchester
Mersey
Montrose

Newcastle
Norfolk
Northumberland

Nottingham

Ocean

Pembroke
Penzance
Portland

Raider
Ramsay
Roebuck

St Albans
Scott
Severn
Sheffield
Shetland
Shoreham
Somerset
Southampton

Tyne

Westminster

York

Branches/Categories

First World War

A – Clerical/Accountant
B – Household
C – Garage Workers
D – General Unskilled
E – Postal
F – Miscellaneous
G – Technical
H – Signal Branch

Category A
Clerical
Ledger Clerks
Shorthand Typists
Typists
Victualling Stores Assistants

Category B
Butchers
By-products Women
Cooks
Domestics
Laundresses
Stewards

Category C
Despatch Riders
Driver Mechanics
Vehicle Washers

Category D
Messengers

Orderlies
Packers
Porters
Storewomen

Category E
Sorters (Postal)
Telegraphists
Telephonists

Category F
Bakers
Depth-charge Primers
Gardeners
Lamps (Repair/Maintenance)
Net Mine Workers
Pigeon Women

Category G
Acetylene Welders
Aeroplane Plate Fitters
Armourers (Air)
Bolt Driller/Pin Fitter
Canvas Stitcher
Carpenters
Cleaners
Coppersmiths
Cutter Grinders
Cylinder Capper/Valve Grinder
Draughtswomen
Drillers/Fliers
Fabric Workers
Fitters
Gun Cleaners (Air)
Hand Capstan Lathe Workers
Instrument Repairers

Instrument Winders
Instrument Workers
Jig-saw, Hand-saw, Rib/Strut Makers
Machinists
Magneto Repairers
Photographers
Piston Scraper/Part Cleaners
Plane Cylinder Car Grinder
Plumbers
Respirator Repairers
Sailmakers
Shaping Machinists
Storekeepers I (technical knowledge)
Storekeepers II (no technical knowledge)
Tinsmiths
Tracers
Upholsterers
Wing Workers
Wiring Hands

Category H
Signal Women
Wireless Telegraphy Operators

Officers' Branches
Accountant
Administrative
Anti-Gas
Assistant Paymaster
Cypher
Fleet Mail
Intelligence
Medical
Quarters
Secretarial
Signals

1939–45

Accountant/Sub-Accounts Officers
Administration Officers
Aircraft Checkers
Aircraft Engineer Officers
Aircraft Recognition Officers

Air Mechanics (O) (Ordnance)
     (L) (Electrical)
     (E) (Engines)
     (A) (Airframes)
Air Radio Officers

Air Raid Protection Officers
Air Synthetic Trainers
Amenities Liaison Officers
Amenities Liaison Ratings
Analysers (S) (Gunnery)
Anti-Aircraft Calculators
Anti-Aircraft Target Operators
Anti-Gas Instructors
Armament Stores Officers
Armourers
Automatic Morse Transcribers
Battery Chargers
Blacksmith
Boarding Officers
Boat Drivers
Boat's Crew
Bomb Range Markers
Boom Defence
Censor Officers
Cine-Gun Assessors
Cinema Operators
Classifiers (Special Writers/Linguists)
Coders
Coders (s)
Cooks (o) (s)
Cypher Officers
Cypher Ratings
De-Gaussing Recorders
DEMS (Pay)
DEMS Inspection Officers
Despatch Riders
Dome Operators
Drafting Officers
Drawing Duties
Duty Staff Officers
Education Officers
EVT Instructors
Exercise Officers
Fabric Workers
Fighter Direction Officers
Flying Control Officers
Gardeners
Gunnery Experimental Assessors

Gunnery Experimental Officers
Hairdressers
Hall Porters
Instructional Film Officers
Intelligence Officers
Laundrymaids
Linguists
Linguists (Special Duties)
Maintenance
Maintenance (Air)
Medical Officers
Mess Catering Officers
Messengers
Meteorological Officers
Meteorological Ratings
Minewatchers
Motor Transport Drivers
Net Defence
Night Exercise Attack Teachers
Night Vision Test Officers
Orthoptists
Parachute Packers
Personnel Selection Officers
Photographers
Photographic Assistants
Plotting Officers
Plotting Ratings
Press Officers
Printers
Qualified Ordnance (Air)
Qualified Ordnance (Combined Operations)
Qualified Ordnance (Light Craft)
Quarters Assistants
Quarters Officers
Radar Operators
Radio Mechanics (Air) (Air Radar)
Rangefinders
Recruiting Assistants
Recruiting Officers
Regulating Ratings
Routeing Officers
Safety Equipment Assistants
Safety Equipment Officers

Secretarial Officers
Ship Mechanics (Light Craft)
Ship Recognition Officers
Shorthand Typists
Signal Distribution/Despatch
Signal Exercise Correctors
Signallers
Signals Officers
Stewards (g) (o) (s)
Submarine Attack Teachers
Supply (Air Stores)
     (Clothing)
     (Naval Stores)
     (Victualling)
Tailoresses
Telephone Operators
Teleprinter Operators

Topographical Officers
Topographical Ratings
Torpedo Attack Assessors
Torpedo Attack Teachers
Torpedo Ratings
Victualling Officers
Visual Signallers
Welfare Officers
Welfare Workers
Wireless Telegraphy Instructors
Wireless Telegraphy Operators
Writer (D) (overseas dockyards only)
Writer (General)
     (Pay)
     (Pay) (DEMS)
     (Pay) (Royal Marines)

1947–90

Aircraft Direction Officers
Aircraft Engineering Mechanician
Aircraft Engineering Officers
Aircraft Mechanician
Air Stores
Air Traffic Controllers
Cinema Operators
Communications Officers
Cooks (o) (s)
Dental Hygienists
Dental Surgery Assistants
Education Assistants
Education and Training Support
EVT Instructors
Family Services
Fleet Analysis Officers
Hairdressers
Instruction Officers
Mess Caterer
Meteorological Officer
METOC Rating (Meteorological)
Motor Transport Drivers
Naval Airwoman

Operations Officer
Personnel Selection Officers
Photographers
Photographic Interpretation Officers
Physical Training Instructors
Public Relations Officers
Quarters Assistants
Quarters Officers
Radar Plotter
Radio (AR) (AW)
Radio Electrical Mechanic
Radio Electrical Operator
Radio Operator
Radio Operator (Morse)
Range Assessor
Regulating
Sick Berth Attendants
Signals
Staff Officers
Stewards (o) (g)
Stores Accountant (v) (c) (s)
Supply & Secretariat Officer
Switchboard Operator

Tailoress
Telegraphist
Telephonist
Victualling Officer
Weapons Analyst

Welfare Worker
Writer (General)
    (Pay)
    (Shorthand)

Post-1996

The WRNS was disbanded in 1993 and all naval categories are now open to women with the exception of those in the Submarine Service, the Royal Marine Commandos and Mine Clearance Divers.

Ratings:

Warfare Branch:
Above Water Warfare
Communications
Electronic Warfare
Survey Recorder
Underwater Warfare

Engineering Branch:
Air Engineer Mechanic
Engineering Technician
Marine Engineering Mechanic

Supply & Secretariat Branch:
Chef
Steward
Stores Accountant
Writer

Medical Branch:
Dental Hygienist
Dental Surgery Assistant
Laboratory Technician
Medical Assistant
Medical Technician
Naval Health Inspector
Pharmacy Dispenser
Physiotherapist
Radiographer
Registered Mental Nurse

Fleet Air Arm:
Naval Airman (Aircraft Handling)
Naval Airman (Met. and Oceanography)
Naval Airman (Survival Equipment)
Photographer

Others:
Divers
Family Services
Recruiting Assistants
Regulating
Royal Marine Bandsman

Officer Branches:
Aircraft Controller
Aircrew Officers
Air Engineer
Barrister
Chaplain
Dental
Executive
Hydrographic Survey
Instructor
Marine Engineer
Medical
Mine Warfare and Clearance
Observer
Pilot (Fixed wing and rotary)
Principal Warfare Officer
Supply & Secretariat
Weapons Engineer

INDEX